R.E.P.O. Your Job

4 Steps To Taking Back Your Future Through Career Change

By Richard N. Stephenson

This book will cover the 4 Step R.E.P.O. process to changing careers. The goal is to help unfulfilled, but employed, folks find and transition to a new, more fulfilling job.

TABLE OF CONTENTS

Published by RichardStep.com Publishing.

Print Edition
http://richardstep.com

Introduction

Do you remember when you were fresh out of school and eager to start your first "real" job? You carefully chose your clothes for your first day, and maybe even got a new haircut. You were looking forward to meeting new people, gaining new experiences and making a good salary.

Dreams of that first car, that new home, and even a beach vacation filled your mind. You couldn't wait to get to work to earn all that. You were on your way to your own piece of the American Dream and it felt great.

Fast forward a decade or so...

You look around you, and you know you *should* be glad you have a good job.

But colleagues and friends have been laid off left and right, several businesses in your community have closed their doors, and some of your friends have even had to give up their homes to foreclosure.

"I should be content," you mutter to yourself. "I have a good job, and I can take care of my bills." But something is missing. That American Dream is starting to feel more and more like a nightmare.

Your job doesn't feel like it's going anywhere. The energy and enthusiasm you used to feel at your workplace now feels routine and forced. You feel like you keep doing the same things repeatedly.

You take some time off to get away and to refresh yourself, thinking that maybe you're just tired. Away from the office, though, instead of concentrating on your approach to that lingering project at work, you find yourself daydreaming about other things.

Maybe it's about that volunteer project that you wish you didn't have to keep putting off. Maybe it's about that new business idea that you keep turning over in your mind. Maybe it's about an ad for that online course that has you thinking about going back to school.

You begin to wonder, "What if I was able to turn that volunteer gig into a job? What if I could make a go of that idea I've been kicking around for my own business? What if I went back to school to get that other degree? What if.....?"

Transform Your "What If" to "What's Next?"

If you find yourself mulling over the idea of launching a second career, you are not alone. The America that was once filled with workers staying at the same workplace for their whole careers has shifted. For more and more of us, a mid-life career change is a viable and desirable way to refocus and re-energize our lives.

The shift has been caused by economic, technological and lifestyle changes of the early 21st century. Maybe you're tired of waiting for the axe to fall as the latest round of downsizing hits your company.

Perhaps you are itching to take advantage of the opportunities the internet affords you to start your own web-based business. Or maybe you are simply feeling burned out by your current career and are longing for more fulfillment in your work.

Whatever your motivation, you can take back your future. With proper planning, you can re-direct your life and launch a whole new career - one that will give you the fulfillment and challenge you are seeking.

It's Time To R.E.P.O. Your Job

You are about to embark on a journey to REPOsses Your Job. It's time for you to take back what is rightfully yours and start living your life on purpose. Here's a run-down of the simple 4-step R.E.P.O. process to *repossess* your career and future:

Step 1: **Realization** - understanding what's really going on.

Step 2: **Exploration** - safely figuring out what will work for you.

Step 3: **Preparation** - getting your ducks in a row.

Step 4: **Ownership** - committing to doing what works best.

If you're ready to get more out of everything you do professionally, then it's time to grab the wheel and steer this career just the way you want. Let's get started!

Step 1

Realization

"Understand What's Really Going On"

Your Goals For This Step:

- Determining if it's really time for a change
- Discovering strengths, personality, and abilities
- Assess accomplishments and realize goals

~~~~~

Timing, or the lack of it, can make or break a successful second career. We hesitate to make a big move, hoping for some unmistakable sign that it's the right time.

We make excuses such as, "Well, if I get this promotion, then I'll know I should stay."

Or "I'll wait until the kids are 18 until I do something." Or "I'll just finish this next project and then I'll let them know I'm leaving."

Or _____ ...you fill in the blank.

The point is we get scared.

Instead of thinking those positive "What ifs," we fill our minds with negative "Oh noes!" "What if I my new business never gets off the ground? What if I never make any money?" In other words, we keep asking ourselves about possible failures. This is a depressing trap!

What's the way out of it? How do you determine if it's the right time for a career change? How do you know whether it's the right move to make the next leap?

It's time to take a long, hard look at yourself.

A Stable Personal Life

First, let's think about the stability of your personal life. If you wait for things to become "perfect" in your life, you'll be waiting for a very long time. You ideally want to make a career move when things are relatively stable in your relationships. If you are about to get married or have a baby, for example, the added stress of a career move could be too much for you.

Similarly, if you are expecting a new career to "fix" things in your personal life, you're headed for some disappointments. Look for ways to strengthen the relationships that are separate from your job.

That is not to say, however, that when you feel better about yourself by moving forward with a new career, that it will not have a positive effect on your family and friends. Just let that positive growth be a product of the change happening inside of you, not a reason for it.

Discuss your ideas for your career with your partner and a few close friends or family members. Their support and encouragement in the early stages can go a long way to making your dream a reality.

Keep this small group apprised of your plans and ask for their feedback. When you are stepping into uncharted waters, it is always a good idea to have people who will be there for you to provide positive feedback, encouragement and constructive criticism.

Your Current Job

Secondly, take a look at the status of your current job. You don't want to burn any bridges there, so think about how you can time your departure to the best advantage of all concerned.

- Do you need to complete a big project before you leave?
- Will you need to train your replacement?

Keep in mind that when you leave on good terms, you can build upon your current work relationships to start your new career. You never know who will benefit you later as a mentor or as a client.

Also, consider if there are some skills you can still learn on your current job that you will need for your new career. For example, you may find that your second career will benefit if you wait until you complete a new level of certification at your current place of employment.

Are Your Finances In Order?

Next, do you have the financial means to make a career change now? In the theater world, there's an old anecdote in which a director tells a young actor who has just auditioned for a big part, "Don't give up your day job."

While it's hard to hear, it makes sense. Don't quit your current job until you have carefully evaluated your financial situation.

According to a MetLife Foundation and Civic Ventures survey of 2,500 people who switched careers, a mid-life job transition takes an average of **18 months**.

About 25% of the survey respondents admitted that they *earned no income* during the transition period, and nearly four out of five of those respondents said that lean transition period lasted at least six months.

Personal finance writer Kerry Hannon, who wrote the book *Great Jobs for Everyone 50+,* says that the two key elements to consider before you bail out of a salaried job to start a new venture are:

1) The state of your finances
   and
2) Your tolerance for risk.

Once you have made the decision to make a career change, you can put a plan into place that will keep you solvent for as long as possible. However, you may need to stay at your current job while you build up the capital you need for your new business venture.

You also may need to cut down on your current expenses and cut corners wherever you can to save money. Be realistic about how much money you need and draw up a clear budget that will get you where you want in as little as time as possible.

Plan out a timeline for your move that takes into consideration your finances, your schedule and a realistic view of how long it will take to make a go of this new job if all goes well.

Think about the long haul and dismiss any ideas of a "get rich quick" scheme.

Your Strengths And Abilities

Now, let's look at your strengths and abilities. Launching a second career doesn't have to mean starting completely over. You can brainstorm ways that you can use your personality and the skills you have already developed in your work experience so far.

Let's begin with your personality.

Someone who is ready for a career change is someone who is ready to leave a safety net. Are you a bit of a risk taker? Maybe at least just a little bit? Good. It's time to fulfill a dream or a passion you may have had for a long time.

The story of Julia Child can be a great encouragement. You've probably heard of Julia - between her book *Mastering the Art of French Cooking* and her ground-breaking TV show "The French Chef," she became a household name.

"I had a big copper bowl and a giant whisk and I beat some egg whites and people had never seen anything like that," Child, who had a quirky and lovable sense of humor, said in a 2002 interview with ABC News.

What you may not know about Julia Child is that her cooking success was the result of a mid-life career change. Yup. Her first career was as a **spy** during World War II. Julia joined the Office of Strategic Services (OSS), the forerunner of the CIA, and was sent undercover to Ceylon (currently Sri Lanka) to work as a file clerk with top security clearance.

While there, Julia met her future husband, OSS employee and diplomat Paul Child, and she moved with him to Paris. Looking for something to pass her time, Child, who was 37, followed her passion by enrolling at the famous Cordon Bleu cooking school.

"I was able to enter something I really wanted," she said during the interview. Julia Child's life and career is a testament to the idea that it is never too late to start another career. A strong, adventurous, and playful personality just might be the extra oomph needed in your career growth.

Persistence Is As Persistence Does

Another characteristic of someone who is ready to make a career change is persistence. If you are looking for overnight success in your second career, you are setting yourself up to fail. Good things take time and hard work, but the benefits are worth it.

Author Gray Basnight was laid off from his job as a business radio reporter when he was 45.

While the timing of his second career was unplanned, Basnight used the time he had on his hands to work full-time on a Civil War novel he had been working on sporadically for a few years.

After finding that historical fiction is a difficult genre for a new author to get a publisher's attention, Basnight wrote another novel called *The Cop with the Pink Pistol* in six months and was able to get it published by Ransom Note Press. With that book published, he is now on his way to getting his Civil War book in print.

"Failure is not an option," Basnight said in an interview with The Huffington Post. "Even if the historical novel never sees print - the next manuscript, or the next manuscript, or the next manuscript - will!"

Okay, you're ready and willing to take the second career plunge. Now it's time to assess your skills and to see which of your strengths can translate into a thriving job.

Identifying Your Skills

If you have been in the workforce for five or more years, you have already developed a set of skills that can be transferred to a variety of tasks. You may need to repackage them, but once you are aware of them, you can confidently put them to work in a variety of on-the-job ways.

An added bonus of going through the self-assessment process is that you will be able to identify any weaknesses you need to strengthen before embarking on your second career. We'll do this manually at first, but automated tools are mentioned later in the book. Do both!

Okay, you're going to need some good old-fashioned pen and paper for this task. Let's start with two broad headings: *specialized* skills and *general* skills.

Think about your current and past jobs and any volunteer jobs you have had and begin brainstorming what you have learned and accomplished. Specialized skills would be ones that fit into a specific career, and general skills are ones that can be adapted to any career setting.

For example, if you have knowledge in computer languages and scripts such as Java or JavaScript, list those under specialized skills. You also can list any specialized training and certificates you have earned under the Specialized heading.

Now think about your general skill set. Examples are problem solving, creativity, ability to work as part of a team, organizational skills, leadership, critical thinking, and salesmanship.

Are there certain skills in this set that you can break down into subsets?

If one of your general skills is communication, for example, can you add "public speaking" experience or "report writer?"

Don't forget about the skills you have developed as a volunteer.

That fund-raiser you ran for your son's school or that team you coached for the local Boys and Girls Club can provide valuable experience for your new career. You may even be able to transfer a skill you have developed as a hobby into a full-blown second career.

Self-Assessment: Automated

Now that you've been through the ringers of doing a self-assessment manually, it's time to make things a bit easier. I've created several self-tests that are available at richardstep.com. All of them take between 5 to 15 minutes to complete and cover topics from personality, motivation, strengths, and communication styles.

I suggest taking all of these tests when you have a few minutes to spare. Shortly after reviewing your results, determine to use those insights in your career change journey. The results will give you confidence, insights, and even the right terms to use during your adventure. Here's the list:

1) **Strengths and Weaknesses Aptitude Test**
2) **DOPE 4 Bird Personality Test**
3) **Jungian 16 Types Personality Test**
4) **Self Motivations Quiz**
5) **Small-Talk / Workplace Communications Test**

All available at the following link:

http://richardstep.com/self-tests/

Zagat's Career Change

Tim and Nina Zagat were corporate lawyers when they first started printing their namesake restaurant guides. When they both had worked in Paris, the husband-wife team compiled their own list of Parisian restaurants and took this idea for a restaurant ratings guide back home with them to New York.

The very first Zagat guide was published in 1982 and included ratings for 121 New York restaurants. Although the guide barely broke even the first year, an article about it in *New York* magazine stimulated interest and by 1985, that initial guide was selling 40,000 copies per year.

The Zagats eventually quit their jobs to devote themselves full-time to their expanding enterprise, which grew to include guides of hotels, restaurants and nightspots in more than 100 countries.

"We were doing the first user-generated content years before anyone coined the term," Tim Zagat said in a 2009 interview with Forbes magazine. "The first big challenge we had to overcome was being told 'NO!' by every major publisher in New York. Nobody thought people would want to hear what other people had to say about restaurants."

And how did that hobby-turned-second-career work out for the Zagats? Pretty well, I should say. Internet giant Google purchased Zagat in 2011 for a reported $125 million.

Do whatever you do to such a degree that others will appreciate and value your efforts. Do it often enough and you'll be set for life. Find your skills, build them up, and keep on chugging. And for goodness' sake, make sure you're working on important goals.

Setting Your Goals

Now it's time to think about setting some realistic goals for your second career. When you started your first career, you probably had some specific plans.

Maybe you were excited about starting on the ground floor of a company and working your way up the corporate ladder. Maybe you made it a goal to learn the ins and outs of your business.

The trouble is, now that you've done that, you are ready for a new challenge. It's time to redefine your goals.

Many people who are launching a second career are at a point in which they look at life though a different lens. Perhaps you've had your fill of corporate America and are ready to work for a non-profit company. Or, after volunteering with children, you now have a passion to teach full-time as your career.

Get out another piece of paper and list your short-term and long-term goals.

A useful approach to setting specific goals is to follow the SMART model created by George Doran, Arthur Miller and James Cunningham. In an article published in *Management Review* in 1981, these time management experts said that career goals should be.

Note: the 'SMART' terms have seen some revisions over the years and what follows is what usually works best for most folks.

Specific - by targeting a specific area for improvement.

Measurable - by quantifying or suggesting an indicator of progress.

Attainable - choosing goals that are within reach but are still a stretch.

Relevant - by deciding what matters most to achieving your current goals.

Time-Bound - by setting a reasonable deadline to stay on track. Go ahead; make an estimate of when you could be on your way with this new enterprise. Keep in mind all the details you need to complete first and then set a target date. Setting that date can help you put all your plans into perspective.

I also suggest adding the super-charged version of the SMART goals to your toolbox. It's called the SMART and RED-E method. The address below takes you to an article where I explain it in detail and link a useful downloadable cheatsheet.

http://bit.ly/rssmartrede

Here are some questions to consider for setting clearer goals:

Where do I want to work?

Is the idea of working from home appealing to you? Look for ways to base your business out of a home office or to blend an on-site job with telecommuting.

What hours am I willing to put in each week?

Launching a new career may take same heavy-duty effort at the outset. Are you willing to work evenings and weekends to get things off to a lucrative start?

Do I need any further education to get started?

Many colleges and universities offer online enrollment options with flexible hours that could get you started while you are still employed at your current job.

Whom do I know I could ask for advice?

Don't underestimate the value of a mentor as you embark on this new path. Identify someone you know who has "been there, done that" and set up a meeting to get some advice.

Do I want to be my own boss?

For many Americans, the dream includes being the boss. In a recent poll of 18- to 34-year-olds, for instance, the Kauffman Foundation found that 54% of respondents either wanted to start their business or had already done so. If this is your goal, you need to develop a strong business plan.

What kind of help do I need?

Will you be able to staff this venture yourself or will you need a group of employees? Are you ready to wear many hats in the start-up phase?

What are my space requirements?

Many successful businesses - including Apple, Google and Facebook - started out small in someone's garage or dorm room and grew in size and scope as the business took off. How can you keep your overhead low while you get started?

~~~~~

Really mull over these questions and spend some time understanding just how powerful the SMART goal setting methods can be. Align your actions with the future you want to have. Get some goals that matter and make them happen.

Realizing Your Goals

If you're like most of us, just the act of writing out your career goals on paper makes them seem more real and attainable. To get even more clarity, you might want to take a free assessment quiz online. There are many sites that offer tests to help you decide how well suited you might be to your new career. Here are a few examples to get you started:

1) The **Princeton Review** has a free five-minute career aptitude test that offers hundreds of aptitude profiles, listing all the strengths required for each job. You need to register with an e-mail address and a password, but you do not need to provide any other information to take the quiz.

http://www.princetonreview.com/

2) With the University of Missouri's **Career Interests Game** at, you will discover the six color categories that represent career aptitudes: realistic, investigative, artistic, social, enterprising, and conventional. When you play the game, you find out which career aptitude persona fits you. You might find you are a combination of two personas.

http://career.missouri.edu/career-interest-game

3) Another good web resource for career goal setting is **jobhuntersbible.com**. Hosted by Richard Bolles, author of the popular career book *What Color is Your Parachute*, the site features links to career assessment tests and career goal setting information.

4) There are also several **free self-assessment tests** available on my website. Find your personality, top motivators, top strengths, and communication grade. Hopefully you did most of them already, but there are a few more listed at the address below that I didn't mention earlier.

http://richardstep.com/self-tests/

When you take a couple of these tests and get the revealing results, it can be just the shot in the arm you need to take the next big step into repossessing your future with a brand new career. Are you ready?

Step 1 Review Questions

Q1: What are 2 financial key points you should understand before changing careers?

Q2: Famous chef and TV personality Julia Childs started off with what kind of job before changing careers?

Q3: When cataloging your skills and abilities, what are 2 main types of skills you should divide them into?

Q4: What are the terms that make up the 'SMART' in the SMART goal setting method?

Q5: What are the terms that make up the 'RED-E' in the SMART & RED-E goal setting method?

~~~~~

When you are ready, the answers are on the next page.

Step 1 Review Answers

A1: The current state of your finances (and if you have enough), your tolerance for risk

A2: She was a spy for the Office of Strategic Services (OSS)

A3: Specialized skills, general skills

A4: Specific, measurable, attainable, relevant, time-bound

A5: Reward, ecology, degrees, evaluate

Step 2

Exploration

"Safely figure out what will work for you."

Your Goals For This Step:

 - Consider using your current skills in different applications, industries, and positions
 - Understanding informational interviews and the position before doing the work
 - Testing the waters and figuring out what works for you

~~~~~

Now that you have a clearer idea of your strengths and skills, it's time to explore what possibilities are out there for your new career.

Remember that you have a big advantage over your prior job searches: you have real work experience now and you have a wealth of real-life experience as well.

Sometimes this process involves taking a figurative step back to look at yourself as others might see you. Let's consider some ways you can re-purpose or transfer your current skills and work experiences to a different career path. Several industries are listed next along with ideas for repurposing their characteristic skills.

Real Estate

The economic downturn has hit real estate brokers hard. Have you decided you have hung on long enough and are ready for a change? Good, because you have some highly transferrable skills.

As a broker, you have developed sales and marketing skills. Did you develop your own web page and logo? Are you accustomed to designing flyers and brochures? You could transfer those skills to a second career in advertising or web-based development.

Real estate brokers are also used to working independently, so you are well suited to a web-based freelancing career. Here are some places to get started on this path:

- http://www.guru.com
- http://www.fiverr.com
- http://www.elance.com
- http://www.iwriter.com
- http://www.odesk.com
- http://www.mturk.com

Banking and Finance

Sure you're good with numbers, but you have developed many other skills from your banking career. Here are a few examples to consider: interpersonal and communication skills from dealing with clients, customers and co-workers; analytical and problem solving skills; computer programming and application skills; and personal financial counseling.

Now think about what you liked best about your job. Did you always feel great when you lined up a loan for a customer? You could have the makings of a career counselor or life coach. Were you the "go-to" person office workers asked to help them learn how to run a new computer program? Maybe you should consider software development or higher-tier customer support?

Here's a great free "learn to program" website to check out:

http://www.codecademy.com/

Retail

Let's say you have spent your work life thus far in retail. You started as a store clerk after school and in the summers and worked your way up to management.

The shaky economy has left you either without a job or continually waiting for the axe to fall.

Friends have told you about openings that come up here and there at other retail organizations, but you don't want to make a lateral move to another store. You want out. However, you feel stuck. "I've only done retail," you tell yourself. "That's all I know."

Think again!

Retail involves much more than knowing a product or the way a store does things. Working in retail requires strong communication skills and people skills. You also have displayed problem-solving and organization abilities.

What computer systems have you used on the job? See! You have computer skills as well as math and analytical abilities. Have you created any displays for the store that reveal your creative talents?

Now think about the specifics of your store experience. Could you turn your work at a clothing store into a career in fashion design? Could your experience in home furnishings help you prepare for a career as a home decorator?

Maybe the skills you have developed in customer service could open the doors to a career in human resources. Or maybe your combined wealth of experiences can be put to good use teaching other people what you know? Give Udemy a try - it's free and you can instantly become an online educator.

http://www.udemy.com/

Manufacturing

Have you worked for a manufacturer for so long that you feel it is all you know? Your transferable skills probably include quality control and evaluation as well as time management and organizational abilities.

Don't think that you only have knowledge specific to one trade. You can use the supervisory skills you have honed at your current company to any other company. People are people after all and the hardware always changes.

Your attention to detail, dedication to delivering on-time and safe results, and willingness to work a plan to completion are excellent skills that will serve many other industries very well.

Construction

How can you take your skills and move them into a new job? The building trend of "going green" has not fully reached its potential.

Do you have knowledge of energy-efficient ways to build homes and businesses? There could be options for a new career there.

You also have management skills, planning and scheduling abilities, and probably quite a bit of experience in logistics and problem-solving. Do you have design skills that could transfer to a new field? Consider computer design. Helping people solve design problems before they happen is a huge hole that needs to be filled.

Not-for-Profit

Many not-for-profit organizations have had to cut back their staffing due to the recession. If you have some years of experience working for one of these organizations, however, you are probably used to wearing many hats. This flexibility and knowledge will serve you well in a second career.

Perhaps you have handled a fund-raising campaign or done some special event planning that could work well in an event coordinator job, for instance.

What about a teaching career in the area that your non-profit specialized in? You already have quite bit if knowledge and expertise in that area. Maybe all you need is your teaching certificate to establish a new career.

~~~~~

A large component of successfully launching a new career is to look at yourself in a new way. Get out of the rut of thinking of yourself as being defined by your former job - such as a "retail manager" or a "real estate agent." You are an individual with a broad skill set that can be applied to a variety of endeavors.

Understanding Informational Interviews

Okay, now you are starting to see the broad possibilities that are out there, but you are a little uncertain if a certain new career is right for you. A good next step is to set up a few *informational interviews*.

Richard Bolles, the author of *What Color Is Your Parachute,* describes this process as "trying on jobs to see if they fit you." Most people choose a career direction without taking the time to research the field or to speak with professionals in that field. As a result, they end up in a profession that is not a good match for their skills or interests.

In an informational interview, you meet and talk with someone of your choosing to gain an insider's point of view on a certain career. An informational interview helps you to learn what a certain profession looks like from someone doing it right now.

It also may help you to develop a job search strategy by providing you with a set of suggestions on how to gain knowledge of the skills you need for a profession.

As an added bonus, an informational interview is a valuable form of networking. According to the U.S. Bureau of Labor Statistics, at least 70% of all jobs are found through networking. If you find that you and this new contact person hit it off, he or she might be great help to you as a mentor down the road.

Not only can a mentor help you learn more about your career, but he or she can point you in the direction of other networking contacts, guide you in your specific job search and direct you to opportunities of which you might not have thought.

Finding The Right People

How do you go about finding people to interview?

- Ask friends and colleagues for recommendations and introductions
- Use your university alumni network
- Use social networking sites such as LinkedIn
- Attend Chamber of Commerce or community service club meetings

When you have identified a few prospects, contact them to see if they can meet with you to talk about their work. Be direct. Explain your purpose and your goals and stress that you are seeking information about the profession. You don't want to put anyone in the uncomfortable position of telling you they aren't hiring anyone.

If a contact is receptive to the idea, set up a meeting time at her convenience. Remember she is doing you a favor, so be patient and willing to work around her schedule. Where should you meet? Again, this is up to the other person's convenience. You could suggest that you meet her at her office or you could arrange to meet at a mutually convenient coffee shop.

Be Prepared And Make It Valuable

Before the interview, do your homework. Find out what you can about that person and her position so that you can ask intelligent, informed questions. Ask your contact how much time she has. A 20 to 30-minute interview is usually about right. Have some specific questions ready. Here are a few to consider:

- How did you get this position?
- What do you like most about what you do?
- What is your typical day like?
- What aspect of your job would you change if you could?
- How do you see this industry changing in the next five years? Ten?
- What professional or trade associations do you recommend I join?
- What print and online publications do you recommend I read to keep up with this field?
- What is unique or different about your company and your position?

Dress appropriately for the interview. It's a good idea to dress the same way you would as if this meeting were a job interview for that specific profession. Make sure your clothes are neat, clean, and modest and that you are well groomed.

Because of possible nervousness, you may find yourself worrying about the next question instead of listening carefully to your contact's answers. One way to guard against this tendency is to jot down some notes while she or he is talking. This will also help you remember the important points of what you have discussed when you review the conversation later.

Use your list of questions as a guide, but be prepared to ask follow-up questions that come up based upon how the contact responds to your questions.

After the interview, be sure to send a formal and well-written thank you note either by e-mail or standard mail. Then follow up on the information this contact provided for you.

You can use the research you did for your informational interviews, and the details your contacts give you, to further develop your knowledge of this career path.

Be on the lookout for any career seminars or workshops in this line of work, too. Use your favorite search engine to find articles and books on the career. Visit your local library for a look at career-related magazines and other periodicals.

After all of your research, you're ready to consider dipping your toes into a new pool to see how it really works.

Testing the Waters

Are you ready for the next step in this adventure? Now it's time to test out your new career. Let's look at ways you can test drive your new career path. Here's an example.

Christine had always wanted to be an artist. Drawing had always come to her as a natural ability and, as a young person, she enjoyed drawing the stately homes and historic buildings that filled her northeastern hometown.

She often gave sketches or small paintings of the homes of friends and family members as holiday gifts.

Christine's parents convinced her that she could not make a living as an artist, however, and she entered the corporate world after college. She did well there and worked her way up to management.

After 15 years or so, she was miserable with the politics of her office and she felt she was barely treading water professionally. In order to lessen the stress, she took an evening watercolor class at her local community college.

Not only did Christine love the class and the way painting made her feel, but her instructor encouraged her that she had real talent and that she could sell her work. Slowly and without leaving her office position, Christine began to brainstorm ways she could make the transition from corporate America to full-time artist.

She joined an artists' group that met weekly at the local art museum. She searched online for ideas and resources, and she met with other artists her teacher recommended that she contact. She found the idea of creating watercolor cards and stationery to be appealing, but wasn't sure if she could make it work financially. "It seemed silly to be thinking about hand-painted cards," she recalls, "I wondered, who sends cards anymore?"

Christine kept pursuing the idea, however, encouraged by her newfound artist friends and by her family who saw how happy she was making art again. Christine unexpectedly found her niche at a community service club meeting.

She found herself at the same table with a woman who worked for a non-profit association that was in the planning stages for its 100th anniversary. The company was interested in having an original painting commissioned of its historic headquarters.

"I couldn't believe it," Christine admits. "She said they wanted to do some notecards and stationery items created to mark the anniversary but didn't know how to go about it."

Christine got the woman's contact information, developed several samples and delivered them to her within a week. When they were met with enthusiastic approval by the non-profit's board of directors, Christine was on her way.

Using her business contacts, her marketing knowledge and her artistic talent, she has developed a successful web-based business in which she creates original artwork for homeowners, business owners and organizations. Christine says she not only has a new career, she has a new lease on life.

"Luck" Happens To Those Who Try Harder

Is Christine's example purely serendipity? Maybe. Is it a case of being at the right place at the right time? Yes, a little of that too. But Christine also had put the wheel for her second career in motion by taking a few important steps.

By taking that community college class, she was able to rekindle her love of painting and, more importantly, find out that others thought she was good at it. Next, she built on that first step by joining a group of artists who further boosted her knowledge and her confidence.

Next, she used networking skills and attending a community service club meeting to make a vitally important contact. Then, she followed up on that meeting with a plan and a full-fledged proposal.

It's important to note that Christine did not quit her "day job" right away. In fact, she worked on her art business during the evening and on the weekends for a little more than a year before she gave her notice at the office. "I needed to be sure I could swing it," she admits. "I didn't want to quit my job only to find out I couldn't afford to pay my bills."

You Can Get Started, Too

How can you test the waters of your second career? Think of some ways you can gain hands-on experience in the field you're interested in without actually entering it yet.

You can fit this testing period around your current work schedule with a little planning.

Seek out a small non-profit that relates to your prospective field. Many of these small organizations have had to cut back on staff and would be grateful for your help as a volunteer. Are you interested in a new career as a web designer? Offer to build a new web page for the organization. Would you like to try your hand as a teacher? Volunteer as a camp counselor or with an after-school program for kids.

As a volunteer, you can meet many different employees at an organization. Of course, you will get to know the volunteer coordinators and other people who help with the same activity you do but you also will get to know the rest of the team of that organization.

If you are interested in fundraising and development, ask to take the development director to coffee, for example.

Don't underestimate the relationships you can establish as a volunteer, both with your fellow volunteers and with whomever you interact in that position. You never know what could happen.

It's Never Too Late To Restart

Kari, 51, had always dreamed of a career in teaching and got her teaching certificate in college. But a booming real estate market and a growing family caused her to switch gears and she became a broker.

When Kari's real estate career went through a severe slow-down, she decided to volunteer at a private elementary school near her home. She helped with whatever was needed and often served as a receptionist or as a tour guide for prospective families.

When one of the teachers took maternity leave, the school offered the temporary teaching position to Kari. She was able to prove herself to the administration, to the staff, to the students and to herself.

"Now I am the permanent substitute," she says with a laugh. "I'm not making a living in teaching yet, but I have been offered a full-time position for the fall after one of the teachers retires. I can't wait!"

Kari teaches us to keep learning. Consider taking a night class or a weekend seminar. Many colleges and universities have plenty of options to work around a full-time work schedule, and many offer online or hybrid classes for added convenience.

The more you learn about the field you are considering, and how it will work for you, the better you will be able to ascertain if it is right for you. As you go along this path, keep yourself open to new people and potential contacts.

Use this time to educate yourself and to explore the possibilities that are available. You may find yourself, like Christine and Kari, in a position in which you can combine your passion and talent for something with your career path.

Experiment, trust your instincts, learn and grow.

Step 2 Review Questions

Q1: What are at least 2 other professions that could use skills gained in the Retail industry?

Q2: According to the US Bureau of Labor Statistics, what percentage of jobs are found through networking?

Q3: What are at least 3 things you should ask about during an informational interview?

Q4: Kari was a spry 51 years old when she started along her teaching path. What does Kari teach us about career change?

~~~~

When you are ready, the answers are on the next page.

Step 2 Review Answers

A1: Human resources, fashion design, home decorating, teaching online courses

A2: A whopping 70%!

A3: How they got the job, what they like most, what a typical day is like, what would they change, future projections for the industry, what groups or associations to join, what trade publications to review

A4: It's never too late to change, to keep learning, experiment and test the waters safely

Step 3

Preparation

"Get your ducks in a row."

Your Goals For This Step:

- Protecting your environment and designing safety nets
- Creating an action plan and managing your expectations
- Plan to get more skilled before you leap

~~~~~

The scariest part of launching a second career while you are still employed is the fear of failure.

You've probably stayed in your current job for months - maybe years - while you daydreamed about doing something different.

Holding you back are doubts and questions such as these:

 - How will I support my family during the transition time?
 - What if the new job, company, or idea doesn't work?
 - Shouldn't I be content with what I'm doing?
 - I don't want to disappoint my parents, spouse, or kids.

In the back of our heads is the old part of the American Dream in which a company gives a valued employee a gold watch and a big party for working there for 40 years. Maybe your grandfather even received one of those watches, and you remember how proud he was of it. That gold watch, that retirement party - or the image of it - signified a job well done in our society.

Everything is different now.

Because of an evolving global economy and a lingering recession, many companies have replaced retirement parties and gifts with early retirement packages. Many firms can't afford to keep someone like Grandpa around anymore and outsourced his job long ago.

You know this information intuitively, yet your nagging feelings of doubt still linger, right? You should realize, however, that if you don't deal with these doubts head-on, you *will* stay stuck where you are.

Since you have read this far, you recognize that you have the skills and the knowhow to make this career change a successful venture. What we are looking for now is the mental preparation -- the guts, maybe -- to make the transition.

A Strong Network Of Support

Let's take a few minutes to consider your support network. If you are married, it is essential that you have the support of your spouse to launch this new venture. If you haven't talked about this idea with your spouse, it's time to do that now.

This decision will affect both of you and, of course, any children you have. Here are some steps to guide you in this conversation:

1. Speak clearly and directly about what you want to do and why. Explain that this is not an emotional decision or an automatic reaction but something you have already given a lot of thought to.

2. Share resources and other information you have gathered on this profession with your spouse and answer any questions he or she has.

3. Discuss a potential timetable for leaving your current job and any financial concerns that come up.

4. Explain the non-financial benefits of the new job to you and your family. Better hours? More time at home? Less stress? More creativity?

5. Listen to your partner's concerns. *Really* listen - that includes body language, tone of voice, and reactions over the following days.

6. Be prepared to give your partner frequent updates as your plan moves forward and to keep listening to his or her suggestions.

There's an excellent chance that this proposed change will not come as a complete surprise to your spouse. If you are like most of us, you have complained a little about your current situation and shared your dream of a new career already.

Once you have allayed financial worries, you spouse will realize how much happier you will be when you are doing what you want to do and will welcome the decision.

And About The *Other* People

What about your friends and your family? While it is important to receive as much support as you can, be prepared for a few people - and maybe even ones you least expect - to be critical of your decision.

Your parents are more ingrained in the "gold watch" era and may be worried about your financial security. You may have a few friends who think you are crazy to leave the safety net of a paying job and urge you not to do it.

How do you deal with these doubters? While support from all your friends and family would be great, the reality is the old saying that "you can't please all the people all the time" is true. You may even find that you are doing what they themselves wish they had the courage to do, and that they are a bit jealous. My simple advice: don't worry about it.

Surround yourself with those people who are supportive and encouraging and don't worry about the rest. They may be subconsciously trying to get you down because they don't realize the possibilities ahead. Stay on target!

Forward Action Through Planning

Now you are ready to develop an action plan for your career change. You have already accomplished a great deal by assessing your skills and testing the waters. Now it's time to put your transition into a timetable format.

It's time for you to move past the "I'm thinking about it" stage into the "I'm doing it" phase with a career plan. A career plan is a set of individualized action steps to achieve your goals.

In his book *Selling From the Inside Out,* Barry Siskind explains that we experience two types of setbacks:

(1) Circumstances beyond our control
and
(2) Self-created circumstances.

In order for a career action plan to be useful, you must consider your current circumstances and then develop direct steps that will help you to achieve your goals. In other words, you need to recognize and address any possible deficiencies or limitations that you face.

Here are some questions to address as part of your plan. You can write them and then check them off as you address or complete them. It is helpful to set a deadline for each step whenever possible. A guesstimate is good enough!

 - What do you need to be complete or to accomplish before you give your notice at your current job?
- Do you need to get a second degree or some sort of certification before you make the switch?
- How long will that degree or certification take to achieve?
- How much will that degree or certification cost?
- Do you need to apply for admission or for a scholarship?

- How long will it take to get those application results?
- Do you need to save a certain amount of money to tide you over during the transition period?
- Are you responsible for the completion of any projects at work or for hiring your replacement?

Depending on your particular situation, you will come up with other questions to include as part of your timetable. It's important to be specific and realistic about each step. Don't shortchange yourself on time.

Also, you may need to revise your plan as you go along. Your needs may change or may become more clarified as you complete different aspects of your plan. Be flexible.

Beat Discouragement And Stay Focused

You could start feeling discouraged as you make your list and start thinking that you are far away from your goal. That's where your support group can come in to encourage you. If you have developed a mentor relationship with one of your career contacts, it might be time to give him or her a call.

Keep moving forward by rewarding yourself in small ways as you meet each goal. The reward could be as simple as downloading an e-book on your new career or buying yourself a cappuccino. It could be taking the time out for a long walk or a run in the park.

At some point in this process, you may begin thinking "I'm too old for this" or "I'll be 45 (or 55 or whatever) by the time I get this new career started." In these situations, I often think of an Ann Landers advice column I read long ago.

In the column, a reader who wanted to switch careers to pursue medicine lamented how old she would be in the eight or so years required for medical school, residency and internship. Landers replied, "And how old will you be if you don't?"

Keep taking action steps - even small ones -- in your plan, and you will see progress.

A Zen Path To New Heights

The story of writer Leo Babuata's journey to a second career is an encouraging one. Babauta, who writes the popular "Zen Habits" blog and is the author of the best-selling books *The Power of Less* and *Zen to Done,* was a journalist for 18 years before he changed things up.

The husband and father of six changed many of his life habits and began to chronicle them in a blog, long before blogs were commonplace. His ideas for leading a simplified life struck a nerve with readers, but his transition advice can speak to anyone contemplating a second career.

"First, and most important, I didn't do what I do alone," he explains in a post. *"My wife Eva has made it possible, by supporting what I do from the beginning, by (later) quitting her job and homeschooling the kids (she wanted to do it, but it really helped me), by making sure I have time to work when I need it.*

Second, it didn't all happen overnight. I didn't just quit my job and work from home. I started by finding spaces of time I could use to pursue my passion - waking up earlier and writing for an hour in the morning, writing during my lunch break at work, writing after work for a bit, writing when other co-workers were playing FreeCell (this was pre-Facebook time), writing a bit on Saturdays.

It was important to me, so I made the time...That's difficult for many people, so they don't bother. That means they never find the time to work on their dreams, and they blame their job and family obligations. I was one of those people for a long time. When I finally found the passion ignited inside me, I stopped making excuses and started making priorities. And other than marrying Eva, I've never made a better decision."

What's the take-away from Babuata's example? He had the support of his wife, he didn't quit his job right away but found time to lay the groundwork for his new career, and his success didn't happen overnight.

"Okay, that's a good example," you say, "but Babuata's new lifestyle was still related to his trained career. I'm thinking of jumping into something I have no training or experience in." Here's where you go back to the plan.

How can you gain the experience or training you need for your new career? We've already suggested volunteer work as an option, but what if you need to go back to school?

Education Is At The Tip Of Your Fingers

According to the Bureau of Labor Statistics (BLS), the health care industry is expected to add more than three million jobs by the end of this decade. In addition, the BLS predicts that more than 600,000 computer jobs will be created in the same time.

How can you gain the up-to-date training and expertise you need to launch a career in one of those lucrative fields, for example? The answer is you may need to go back to school. While that may sound daunting, you will definitely not be the only "older" student.

Data from the National Center for Education Statistics (NCES) indicates that roughly 38% of the more than 18 million American college students are age 25 or older. The percentage of all students who are over age 25 is expected to increase another 23% by the year 2019.

The numbers also indicate a shift in what degrees American college students are obtaining, and these numbers point to second careers. Slightly over half of today's college students are seeking a certificate, a credential, or an associate's degree. In 2010, for example, more than a half million students were enrolled in a health sciences certificate program, making it the largest certificate program area.

Okay, you're convinced you won't be the only "old person" in college, but you wonder how will you be able to fit classes in and around your job and all the other demands of your life. Well, along with this influx of older students, going back to school for a new career has caused a change in the way many colleges schedule their classes.

"Traditional" college students who live on a campus at a four-year institution now number no more than about one-sixth of the total college population. 37% of undergraduates are enrolled part-time and 32% work full-time. The non-traditional student, in fact, now outnumbers the typical student, and learning institutions are paying attention by offering a wide variety of options.

Make Learning Work For You

Jenna, 44, realized her job as a fitness-center director was a dead end about six years ago. She developed a plan that enabled her to maintain her job while going back to school to become a physical therapist.

"At the fitness center, I saw the need for physical therapists especially for the older population," she says. "I liked talking with the older folks who came in to the center, and I realized I had my idea for a new career. I just had to make it happen."

Jenna was able to work out a combination of evening, weekend and online classes that she could work around her work schedule at the fitness center. "When there was a class that I had to take on Mondays and Wednesday afternoons, I was able to switch my hours at the fitness center. I just came in earlier on those days. The center opens at 5:30 a.m., so it really wasn't a problem at all."

After she obtained her degree, Jenna kept her manager job while she looked for and interviewed for jobs as a physical therapist. I was used to going to school and juggling my job, so I felt no need to rush things. I'd worked hard, and I wanted to make the best decision I could."

Today, many of Jenna's patients are people she met at the fitness center or their friends. "It took me almost five years from start to finish, but everything eventually fell into place," she admits. "I am so glad I made this change. For the first time in my life, I can really say that I love my work!"

Hustle Through The Bustle

How do you go about seeing what credentials you need for you second career? Go back to your notes from your informational interviews. With some careers, such as Jenna's, there is no way around that extra level of certification, but with others, it is more about experience.

If you do not need to get a degree, explore the possibility of attending workshops or seminars in your field. Is there a way you can gain experience by interning at an office or job shadowing another professional?

According to a survey by CareerBuilder, 23% of employers report that they have internship applicants who have more than 10 years of experience in the workforce. Internships are a great way to test out an employer or a career to see if it is right for you. In fact, often both employer and employee can view an internship as a lengthy and very specific job interview.

Cary Barbor, the host and producer of the podcast *Books and Authors*, wanted to leave her job in the print magazine industry, to follow a dream of a career in radio.

"I put my pride aside and applied, and then counted myself lucky to be chosen to work as an intern - four days a week for five months - at Studio 360, a popular, national radio show that explores creativity and the arts," she writes in her blog.

"Technically, it wasn't unpaid. I was reimbursed about $10 per day. I remember thinking that it was enough for the subway down there and back, or lunch, but not both. But luckily, I had money saved, and had an employed and supportive husband."

"I stayed there - working once a week - for a year or so, until that Executive Producer recommended me for a professional, paying job on satellite radio's Martha Stewart Living channel, which I got."

How Do You Find An Internship?

Many of the internship positions are unadvertised, so it comes back to your networking skills. Search online for groups you can join in your field. In addition to online chat rooms and social media pages, you may find that there are local chapters that meet in your area.

Take the time to attend that group's meetings. Introduce yourself and ask questions about internships or any volunteer opportunities that may be available.

If you aren't able to discover any internships in your field, then think of ways you could suggest one. In today's economy especially, many business owners are open to creative ideas to help their businesses to grow or to get their name out there. Come up with a plan and try it.

Be prepared to handle a variety of tasks and even some grunt work as an intern. The CareerBuilder survey identified the following typical duties for interns:

- Hands-on experience related to career, 73%
- Office support, 52%
- Customer service, 35%
- Office errands, 23%
- Office maintenance, 19%

While you are doing those other tasks, however, you can be learning valuable information about your new profession and meeting people who can help you get started with your new career.

Step 3 Review Questions

Q1: What are at least 3 things you should discuss with a close one (e.g. spouse) before considering changing careers?

Q2: What are 2 types of setbacks you can experience in the career change process?

Q3: What percentage of American college students are 25 years old or older?

Q4: Of the 23% of CareerBuilder employers surveyed, how much experience does the average intern already have?

~~~~~

When you are ready, the answers are on the next page.

Step 3 Review Answers

A1: Be direct and instill confidence in this being a non-emotional decision, share your research thus far, potential timetables for the process, non-financial benefits (more time, less stress, more freedom), their emotions and reactions

A2: Circumstances beyond your control, self-created circumstances

A3: 38% according to the NCES

A4: 10 or more years of professional workforce experience

Step 4

Ownership

"Committing to doing what works best."

Your Goals For This Step:

- Understanding, calculating, and taking risks to get what you want
- Searching and networking to find (and get!) the right job
- Committing to change and then choosing to jump

~~~~~

You've read the stories: a corporate executive becomes a high school teacher, an investment banker starts an internet clothing business, and a marketing executive becomes a software engineer.

More and more Americans are launching second careers. They may be doing it to fulfill a dream.

They may be doing it to earn more money. They may be doing it to be more productive and content.

Nearly 8.4 million Americans between the ages of 44 and 70 have already started second and third careers, according to a survey by the MetLife Foundation and Civic Ventures. Of the workers surveyed who have not already launched a new career, about half of them are interested in doing so.

Are you still wavering? It might be helpful to look at the risk-reward ratio.

'Risk' Is *Not* A Bad Word

You've heard that it can often take money to make money. While it may be true that you will have to invest some time and lost income into starting your new career, the risk may well be worth it.

Instead of just thinking about the transition period and the worry of losing that reliable paycheck, think about what you will be earning on your new career path. You'll find details about the salary range for specific jobs in the Department of Labor's Occupational Outlook Handbook. Visit **http://bls.gov/ooh/** for more details.

If you're heading back to school, look for opportunities for financial aid.

You are eligible for subsidized loans at any age and you are also eligible as a part-time student. Consider the variety of scholarships and grants that are available for older students too.

Visit **http://studentaid.ed.gov/** for ideas or check out sites such as **http://www.fastweb.com/** and **http://www.scholarships.com/** to see what is available for financial help.

You can also take advantage of some educational tax breaks. Depending on your income, you might be able to qualify for a lifetime learning credit, which is worth up to $2,000 each year. If your current income exceeds the limit, you still may be able to deduct tuition and fees, up to $4,000, from your taxes. For details, visit **http://www.irs.gov/** and **http://www.nasfaa.org/**.

Money Might Be Tight, But Happiness Reigns

What if your new salary will take a while to get to what you are making now or what if you will be taking a significant long-term pay cut in order to pursue your dream? It's time to rely on your support network again.

The benefits of working at a job you love - for a philanthropic organization or for your own home-based business, for example - offer benefits of satisfaction and freedom that money can't buy.

You may reap rewards in your health because of being under less stress. You also may save on other real costs such as commuting and wardrobe expenses in your new career. You may find that this new endeavor opens the door to a different lifestyle in fact.

Maybe you'll find you can take public transportation to work or walk to many of your neighborhood errands and will be able to cut down or give up completely the use of your car, for example. Think of the savings in gas, upkeep and insurance that can come from being car-free. That's' what *Zen Habits* writer Leo Babuata did.

Of course, there are even more radical options like selling your house and moving to a smaller home, or even moving to a new part of the country where living expenses are cheaper. That's what Tim, a former investment banker, did. By exchanging living in New York City for Pittsburgh, which is where he grew up and has family, Tim and his wife were able to open their own restaurant.

The point is that with some planning and forethought, you can find other ways to compensate for any lost income caused by your new career.

With Managed Risk Comes Great Reward

We tend to view risk-taking as a negative thing in our society. Taking risks can put us in a position for great opportunity, however.

Heather Rabbatts, a Jamaican-born lawyer who became the first female director of England's Football Association, said in an interview with the BBC, "I think I've always felt that there was something quite exciting about taking risks. And there's a great saying, actually, that you only learn when you are at risk and I'm fascinated by both risk and learning, so that has led me to take jobs that people would think 'you can't do that, that's just impossible.' No it won't be."

When you take a calculated risk, it does not mean there is not preparation involved. The most successful risk takers work hard on their research and their plans and then move forward in the knowledge that they might fail but that they also might succeed.

Jeanne Kucey, who is the CEO of Jetstream Federal Credit Union, said in an interview with the Credit Union Times magazine that risk taking is a form of leadership.

She said, "While I'm definitely a risk taker, at the same time I do my homework and understand the importance of implementation and follow through."

"You can't just throw a bunch of ideas without seeing the whole process of a project and what the end should be or look like. Don't *let* fear rule any aspect of your life."

Safety In Numbers

In addition to networking with people involved with your new career, it can be helpful to connect with others who have made any mid-life career change. You can support each other and exchange ideas. Here are some common ways of reducing the risk of launching a new career:

1. Start off part-time. With even a few hours week, you can get your feet wet in the new field without leaving your current job.

2. Slowly cut back on your hours in your current job while you start working part-time in your new one. Perhaps you could work four days a week in your current job and one day in the new field, for instance.

3. Consider working in your field on a freelance basis from your home computer. This option offers flexibility and low costs. Check out some of the many sites available for freelance work in web-design, writing, editing, translating, tutoring and computer programming. We covered these earlier, but here are the links again:

- http://www.guru.com
- http://www.fiverr.com
- http://www.elance.com
- http://www.iwriter.com
- http://www.odesk.com
- http://www.mturk.com

Job Searches In Today's Market

If you haven't been out in the job hunt arena in a while, you need to get up to speed with current job search culture. There are many services and tools you can use to find and get the right job. Let's look at a few of them.

The days of mailing out resumes and waiting to hear back are long over. Today, you can gain professional contacts and get your resume in the hands of countless employers through social media sites.

If you don't have a LinkedIn account yet, you need to set one up as soon as possible. With LinkedIn, you can create a free, detailed professional profile that includes your resume and portfolio.

A survey from the recruiting site **Jobvite** found that 93% of today's job recruiters search LinkedIn to find qualified candidates, up from 87% last year. Other popular social networking sites are growing in influence with recruiters as well. Facebook is used by 66% of those surveyed, and Twitter is used by 54%.

Embrace Your Maturity And Experience

Instead of selling your inexperience in your new profession short, sell your wisdom and life experience to potential employers.

Many companies will appreciate having someone who is not looking at their company as a stepping-stone but as a new and fresh opportunity. Promote your talent and your multi-faceted background.

Use your social network to discover others who have the same or similar career path as the one you are seeking as your own. Try to find out more about their experiences and about what they are doing now. You may find new and creative ways to link aspects of your job experience with your new path, like combining sales and marketing with software development.

If you see that one of your first-line LinkedIn connections has someone in his network that is involved in your new profession, you can ask him to introduce the two of you through the website. The power of being "linked in" is real.

In addition, search online for discussion forums in your new field. Join these groups to read the conversations and to learn about current topics and trends in the profession. It's still social media, but it's the "old guard" that still has a lot of great stuff to share.

People Still Talk To Each Other?

In addition to social media, look for ways to meet more contacts face to face. Attend professional conferences and receptions. Join civic groups and organizations that draw professionals from your community. Search online for a local chapter of a trade association that focuses on your new career.

You'll be surprised at how many different specialized organizations are out there. Attend a meeting to make new contacts and to gain new information. Many of these organizations have online sites with job leads.

Use your record of accomplishment in your current profession, any volunteer work you have done and your personal group of friends to spread the word that you are seeking a new job in a new field.

You never know who could be the person who makes the difference. It could be a friend from high school you haven't seen in years or an old neighbor. Keep your options open and keep getting your name and your purpose out there.

Mark was able to turn a volunteer job with a non-profit organization that helped people with disabilities gain employment into a new career.

"I helped out at the office because the group had helped my brother get a wheelchair when he needed one," he recalls.

"I noticed a flyer on the bulletin board about an organization for people working in the field of clinical social work," Mark, who was working as the manager of a large restaurant, says. "I decided to go to their next meeting because it was on my day off... I was more and more interested in becoming a social worker, but frankly I was worried about making such a wild career change."

Long story, short, Mark met a few valuable contacts at that first meeting and got details on what he needed to do to make his new career a reality. "That meeting was a real leap of faith for me," Mark admits. "For the first part of the meeting, I didn't even take my coat off because I didn't think I'd be staying."

Sometimes you just have to get out there and get in people's faces. No, not like that. You have to get in front of the cart if you want to catch it and then maneuver your way onto it.

Get Your "You" Papers In Order

After you've spent time analyzing your finances and have done some networking, it's time to create an ideal job description to help you refine your target career.

Be as detailed as you can with this description. Be sure to include how the job would fit into the rest of your life, including your family and hobbies.

That way, hopefully, your next career will provide the fulfillment you're not getting from your current job.

Your next step is to get your resume up-to-date. There are many online templates for re-working your resume to meet today's new standards, which include keywords and online links. Use your favorite search engine to check for many free template options.

If you have no idea where to start, or are looking for another set of "reviewing eyes" to look over your resume, then $5 can bring you some tremendous insights. You'll have to poke around Fiverr for a match that works best for you, but I found several gigs that reviewed, made suggestions, and worked with me to create excellent resumes.

Give the following link a try. It sorts "Resume and Cover Letter" worker "gigs" by user rating. A "gig" is Fiverr's term for a job. You may have to try a few, but what's $5 when it comes to such a huge part of the job hunting process?

Since you are changing careers, it will be best for you to design a functional -- or skill-related -- resume rather than a chronological resume.

Go back to your list of transferable skills and highlight them in a way that shows how your talents and skills fit your new career choice.

With a functional resume, you can focus on the skills you have gained throughout your career rather than on specific job experience. For example, you could list a skill - such as customer service - and then follow it with the many ways you have developed that skill.

Don't just list your responsibilities without showing the results you have achieved. Show what makes you different from other applicants. Use numbers, examples, and tangible proof when possible. Rather than trying to hide the reality that your current job is in another field, embrace it by focusing on your strengths.

Be sure to include your volunteer experience and reveal how it suits this new profession. Don't neglect any college classes, seminars and workshops you have completed. Remember you can also use the people you have met in these endeavors as references.

Culture And Staying Relevant

How do your hobbies or special interests help reveal who you are to a potential employer? Do you coach Little League Baseball? Do you design costumes for a community theater?

Maybe you have a black belt in karate. These interests can help a potential employer see that you are well rounded and interesting.

Do some homework to find out about a particular company's culture. You might find that the owners are actively involved with the community. Perhaps volunteer work you have been doing for years with foster children will help get you noticed.

It's true that a professional resume is not the place to tell everything about yourself as it needs to be brief. But when you share details that reveal how you will fit well into the company's framework, you have a better chance of securing an interview and the job itself.

As you move forward in launching your second career, be sure to keep your resume, your portfolio and your social media accounts current and up to date. Of the more than 8,000 employers surveyed by CareerBuilder recently, half reported that the resumes they received for new job applications had outdated information.

Commitment Is Key - Embrace It

Let's go back to how you felt when you were just embarking on your first career. Did you feel that you could accomplish anything and that you were on the brink of a successful and satisfying career? Do you want to feel that way again? You can.

It's time now to commit to a new career.

When you stop second-guessing yourself and fully decide to move forward with a new career, you will find that many of the roadblocks you thought were in the way will be removed. In other words, you may find that your doubts and insecurities have been the biggest problems in your way.

Time is a big factor that stands in the way of making a commitment to change. You may have had a perceived lack of time in the back of your mind throughout the reading of this e-book, in fact.

Well, you're right. Launching a new career will take some time. But fortunately, you have some; you just need to recoup it. Here are a few sneaky ways to get more time in your life:

Cut down on TV. For many people, this one change will free up a couple hours a day or more. You don't have to go cold turkey. Just eliminate the mindless watching and keep only the best stuff.

Read less junk. You do not need to click on every news article on your internet home page. Try to focus on what is really important and skim or skip the rest.

Get up earlier. It's tough at first, but after your body gets used to it, it gets easier and easier. This tip is especially helpful if you have children at home. You can accomplish quite a bit in a quiet house. Or use the time for exercising. It works! Trust me. Look at "polyphasic sleeping" for a real hack here.

Say "no" more. It sounds harsh, but you have to cut down on social and volunteer commitments in order to make this career change. Simplify your life and you will find that you have more time for what makes you happy.

If you are someone who finds it hard to say no to requests for your time, you will find this difficult at first, but people and the organizations they represent will survive. You can always get back involved with the ones that mean something to you later on.

Bring Your Commitment To Life

Once you have freed up some time in your life, the next step is formalize your commitment to launching this new phase of your life. Try changing the way you have been thinking about it and the words you choose to describe it to reflect your commitment. Here are a few examples:

Instead of saying, "I'm going to give this new career a try," say, "I'm going to make this new career happen."

Instead of saying, "I think I could be good at this," say, "I have developed skills in this area."

Instead of "I will change my career when this happens or that happens," say, "I am ready to make this change in my life now."

When you get accustomed to speaking in positive language about your new career path, it can really change the way you feel about it. You will start to *believe* that you can make it happen. And everyone around you, including any nay-sayers, will too.

Even though we are very near the end of your journey in this book, we are only just getting started. Are you ready to get started?

Step 4 Review Questions

Q1: What are at least 3 ways you can find more "productive free time" in your day?

Q2: How can you safely reduce the risk of launching a new career while keeping your current job?

Q3: Of the social networking sites mentioned in this step, which one does HR use most often to find new prospects?

Q4: What kind of resume should you use if you're entering a brand new field or industry?

~~~~~

When you are ready, the answers are on the next page.

Step 4 Review Answers

A1: Cut down on TV, read less junk, get up earlier, say 'no' more often

A2: Start off working part-time hours, slowly cut back on your current full-time hours (or switch schedules to 9-80), start experimenting with freelance work

A3: LinkedIn @ 93% usage by HR

A4: A functional resume (to focus on accomplishments, not employment time-line)

Conclusion

I hope by this time that you are feeling positive and empowered that you can take the big step of launching a new career. It can feel a little overwhelming to contemplate such a huge change, particularly when, as we have discussed, it involves some risk.

However, if you follow the R.E.P.O. steps we have outlined in this book and add in your own unique purpose, talent, drive and commitment, you will see that making the choice to begin a new career can be the best decision you ever make.

Check over your action plan each day, checking off the tasks you complete and breaking down the larger tasks into smaller ones whenever necessary to keep your momentum going. Reward yourself in small ways when you meet your goals each day.

If you are feeling unhappy in your current job or if you are unemployed, you might be feeling pressure to make a quick change.

Release yourself from that pressure. Remember the timetable you set is up to you. The important thing is to get started and to keep moving forward with your plan.

You can ease slowly into this new career. Take the time to network, to volunteer, to attend meetings, and even to work part-time in your new chosen profession before you commit to it completely.

This period will not only give you valuable experience and help you meet important contacts who may help guide you in the future, but it will also give you the opportunity to gain confidence that you are on the right career path. You can even make some slight detours or changes before working full-time in the new field depending upon what you discover along the way.

Here's a piece of parting advice. Be sure to take care of yourself while you are on this journey. It's easy to feel so busy that you neglect the time you need for yourself -- for daily exercise, proper nutrition, rest and relaxation. When you manage those important areas of your life, you will ensure you have the creative energy and the stamina for the challenges ahead.

The rest of this exciting equation is up to you. Here are some questions to ask yourself:

- Are you ready to feel excited about beginning work each day?
- Are you tired of feeling that your talents and skills are under-utilized in your current job?
- Is it time to get unstuck from a routine that feels stagnant and dull?
- Is a sense of purpose missing in your life?
- Have you found or re-discovered a hidden talent?
- Have you developed skills that come from real-life and from maturity?
- Are you committed to making a positive change in your life that can have a ripple effect on your family?

If you answered "yes!" to these questions, congratulations, you are ready to launch a meaningful and exciting second career. You are ready to take back your job and your life. Let's go through those R.E.P.O. steps one more time.

Step 1: Realization = CHECK!
Step 2: Exploration = CHECK!
Step 3: Preparation = CHECK!
Step 4: Ownership = CHECK!

You are now ready to **REPO**sses Your Future and starting getting more out of your life. But don't go so quickly, my friend! I've got one final test for you.

Ready for the final exam?

R.E.P.O. Final Exam

Q1: What is step 1 of the REPO process?

Q2: What are the 3 main goals of the first step in the REPO process?

Q3: What is step 2 of the REPO process?

Q4: What are the 3 main goals of the second step in the REPO process?

Q5: What is step 3 of the REPO process?

Q6: What are the 3 main goals of the third step in the REPO process?

Q7: What is step 4 of the REPO process?

Q8: What are the 3 main goals of the forth step in the REPO process?

Q9: Why should you REPO Your Job?

~~~~~

When you are ready, the answers are on the next page.

R.E.P.O. Final Exam Answers

A1: Realization - understanding what's really going on

A2: Deciding if it's time to change, discovering yourself, knowing accomplishments and goals

A3: Exploration - safely figuring out what will work for you

A4: Reapplying skills to other industries, knowing informational interviews, testing the waters

A5: Preparation - getting your ducks in a row

A6: Protection and safety nets, actions plans and expectations, getting skilled before leaping

A7: Ownership - committing to what works best for you

A8: Taking calculated risks, searching and networking, committing to change

A9: Because it's time to take back your future and regain control over your life

That's it! Have a successful and focused future!

About Richard N. Stephenson

I'm the elbow grease behind richardstep.com, helping thousands discover more about themselves and their career paths daily. I've published several books on career development, personality testing, optimizing learning, and building strengths. I've also designed online self-discovery and career aptitude tests.

Cancer once knocked me down, the good Lord gave me a second chance, and now I want to help you use yours. I take the old career development fluff and turn it into tools you can use. I live to make resources that are guaranteed to help you in your career-boosting journey.

I live near Houston, TX, with my extraordinary wife, adorable kids, and overgrown backyard.

Please feel free to contact me. I'm always looking for more career and life enhancing tips.

EMAIL: **richard@richardstep.com**
TWITTER: **http://twitter.com/rstephenson_**
VIDEOS: **http://youtube.com/rstephensonable**
ADDRESS:
PO Box 3395
League City, TX, 77574-3395

Books by Richard N. Stephenson

See my **Amazon Author page** for my latest books.

http://bit.ly/rnsamazon/

See my **blog author page** for my latest books overall.

http://richardstep.com/products/

Your Review Counts!

If you enjoyed this book, or got at least one golden nugget of usefulness out of it, would you mind sharing your experience with the rest of the world, please?

A 2 to 3 sentence summary of your thoughts is an awesome gift to others who see it. (I LOVE reading them, too!)

Please leave a review on this book's Amazon page:

http://bit.ly/rnsamazon

I'm an independent publisher and your review means a lot to other people considering this investment. It really does help when you share your thoughts and feelings.

Plus, I like the idea of my kids coming by my author pages in 20 years and seeing what the world had to say. I am forever grateful!

Thank you,
Richard N. Stephenson